ROGER STEVENS

The Journal of Danny Chaucer (Poet)

TED SMART

First published in Great Britain in 2002
by Orion Children's Books
a division of the Orion Publishing Group
Orion House
5 Upper St Martin's Lane
London WC2H 9EA

This edition produced for
The Book People Ltd
Hall Wood Avenue,
Haydock,
St Helens WA11 9UL

'Forming a Band' © Roger Stevens 2001 appears in
Turn That Racket Down edited by Paul Cookson (Red Fox)

ISBN 1 84255 058 6

A catalogue record for this book
is available from the British Library.

Typeset by Deltatype Ltd, Birkenhead, Merseyside

Printed in Great Britain by
The Guernsey Press Ltd, Guernsey, C.I.

To The Pathfinders, who changed their name to The Syndicate – Paul, Lewis, Pete and Roger – wherever they are now. And to Steven Herrick.

Contents

1: WELCOME TO THE YOUTH FACTORY AS A NEW SCHOOL YEAR BEGINS

God Bless the Little Lemmings

Little lemmings
Brand new jumpers
Shoes well shone
Ties neatly tied
Rushing pushing
In confusion
Bushy-tailed
And bright-eyed

Little lemmings
Looking scared
Here comes
The Bogey Man
Makes a grab
For lemming head
Stuff it down
The toilet pan

The Ritual Calling of Names

Cell Block G 1-0-3
Is where you'll find me
Danny Chaucer (poet)
Sitting very quietly
Every day at nine a.m.
Next to nervy Sally Cook
(Where Mrs Taggart put me)
(Embarrassment factor 9 point 9
on a scale of 1 to 10)
(For discussing with Tommy Lock
The sad result of the Forest Match)
(If only she'd sat me next
to Jenny Keane)
and half-listening for my name
on the register
(although it's always
in the same place — third)
(After Lucy Attwood
and Diane Bird)
(It takes some time
because Mrs Taggart
always has a lot
of nothing much to say)
And so I spend the time
here in my head
where Jenny Keane says —
Danny, please take me
To the Forest Game
Danny, sail me to a South Seas Cove
Golden Sands and Burning Sun

Danny, tell me
I'm the only one.
There we have
Our first real kiss ...
D-A-N-N-Y C-H-A-U-C-E-R
A-R-E Y-O-U H-E-R-E
I-N T-H-I-S C-L-A-S-S
O-R S-O-M-E-W-H-E-R-E E-L-S-E ?
Er, I'm here, Miss!

The Down Stairs

Never go **up**
The stairs marked **down**
My best mate Tommy Lock did
Just as Special Needs
Were unexpectedly released
(as in several tons of water
unexpectedly released from a dam)
from History
(Special Needs
having no love of the past)

Luckily, the doctor said,
It was a clean break
And Tommy was soon back at school
With his leg
In a plaster cast

A Cast of Thousands

Tommy's plaster cast says

♫

By hook or by crook
I'll be last on this cast

♫

Michael Owen
Walks on water
(Which upset Tommy
Who's a Chelsea supporter)

♫

It's smashing to have you back

♫

Never give a sucker
An even break

♫

Shake a leg!

♫

I think you're very brave – signed Jenny K
(My heart jumped
when I read this)
(If only I had been
Going up the stairs marked down
Upon that fateful day)

2: SOME THOUGHTS ON GIRLFRIENDS PAST

Paradise Mislaid

As humankind destroys the planet
My thoughts turn frequently to Janet

♬

As rainforests are stripped and land laid bare
I think of Janet in her underwear

♬

As acid rain falls from the sky above
I think of me and Janet making love

♬

What chance has humankind of saving this fair planet?
About the same as I have ever making it with Janet

♬

(Actually her name isn't Janet
but Jenny doesn't rhyme with planet)

Clean Hair Day

At the party
She sat on my lap
I can't remember
Too well
What we did
Or said
Or even what she looked like
But I do remember that her hair
Had the smell
Of washing-up liquid

Communication

I waited for her
By the entrance
To HMV
Got chatting
To the *Big Issue* vendor
About the government
About humanity
About atoms
And the spaces in between
Eventually
Reluctantly, in the end,
I concluded
She had stood me up

My new raggedy friend nodded knowingly
A moment shared
I patted his dog's head
And said farewell
But afterwards I thought
I should have bought
His magazine

Kissing A Goth

I've often wondered
What it would be like
To kiss a Goth
Looking into eyes
Dark shadows
On a vast expanse of snow
Kissing black lips
To a creepy soundtrack
Created in a cave
Where light could never go

I've often wondered
What it would be like
To kiss a Goth at midnight
(as I reach for the light switch
am I turning on or off?)

I've often wondered
What it would be like
To kiss a Goth
The chains that hold her down
Rattling as I pull her close
The glint of steel in her smile
Lips soft as a bat's wing
Her tongue
A stud missile

One Night Stand

She turned off the light
Pulled back the curtains
Sighed at the full moon
Sat beside me on the sofa
And whispered *love*
What do you mean, love?
I asked nervously.
She put her head on my shoulder
Her hair silky on my neck
I could feel her body heat
Through my Nottingham Forest shirt
A knock on the door
Her mum's head peered round
Dad wants to come in now
It's time for the football
Would you like a cup of tea?

3: ROCK FAMILY TREE

Famous Folks

My mum is Madonna
Taught me all she knows
About singing
And the rigmarole of sex
All my mates are famous
(Come to lunch one afternoon
Meet David Beckham
Swoon, girls, swoon)

♪

My dad is Alex Ferguson
Taught me all he knows
About football and winning
Want to meet the Man U team?

♪

Madonna and Alex
Met in Italy
Dad was with Aberdeen then
Playing in a friendly
Against AC Milan
And Mum
Had a day off filming
They had that instant
Sun-bursting-through-the-clouds
Love-at-first-sight thing
And later
Behind the Coliseum
Well ...
Here I am

♪

Alas their love was doomed
Their diaries too full
Madonna had more hits to write
Alex was looking for a challenge

♪

But I still visit them
And they meet up when they can
And send me gifts on my birthday
A signed football
A CD
C/o my adopted parents

Grandma

Grandma was always there
Did she always have silver hair?
Lived next door
But when we visited her in the nursing home
Part of her was missing
Who are you? she asked me.
I told her
Remember, I said, *how we used to*
Go to the market
To buy scraps of silk?
She smiled.
Remember you took me to
The seaside bingo
And I won a dartboard?
She nodded.
Remember me and Grandad
Playing football on the yard
And breaking the shed door?
We both laughed.
And when the bell rang
And the nurse said
It's time to go
I held Grandma's hand
And she said
Who are you?

Uncle Roy

It was Uncle Roy who turned me on
To music
He still has hair down to his shoulders
And wears denim flares
Like in the Seventies
Very trendy, he thinks
He has scant regard for his neighbours
Plays Deep Purple or Led Zeppelin
At about a thousand decibels
Accompanied on his beaten and battered cherry-red
Fender Stratocaster guitar
I loved that sound
And would go round to Uncle Roy's
At every opportunity
And I even grew to like the music
Although not fashionable
I still find it has a certain
Je ne sais quoi

The Academy of Sound

The smell — new, electric, polish, sweat — like no other
Something about the shine of red rosewood
The symmetry of guitars covering the walls
Like an art gallery
Gus (so his badge proclaims)
Plucks, from its stand, a Fender Strat
(As used by Eric Clapton)
(Of whom you may not have heard
Except for his boring, maudlin
Wonderful Tonight song
Listen instead to *Layla*
That rocks!)
(Eric, a guitar hero,
Once thought of as a god by many,
So Uncle Roy says)
(Sorry, I'm going on a bit, I know
Where was I?
Oh, yes ...)
I hold the guitar
In my hand,
Shy, unacquainted
Try a few chords
Nice action, I say, knowledgeably
To Gus, who looks bored
I play a snatch of
Stairway to Heaven
(Watching from the corner of my eye
For some response from other customers,
Like, Wow! That boy can *play*!)
(Gus winces)

Which Led Zeppelin wrote
(Uncle Roy's favourite band)
And say to my father
(Who is staring vacantly into space,
Not bored exactly
but kind of unplugged)
This is the one!
He says, *Are you sure?*
Yes, yes! I'm certain.
He pulls out his credit card
And goes off with Gus to pay.
I hold my new girlfriend in my arms.
We are going to make sweet soul music together
On the Stairway to Heaven

Led Zeppelin's Famous Song

When Led Zeppelin wrote
Stairway to Whitstable
Stairway to Sheerness
Stairway to Cradely Heath
Stairway to Skeggy
Stairway to Marks and Spencer's Men's Dept
Stairway to Sheffield
Stairway to the M25
Stairway to Heaven

To come up with a good title
Took longer than expected
(Stannah Stairlift to Heaven
Was also rejected)

4: MEANWHILE, BACK AT THE YOUTH FACTORY

Miss Potter's Pyrotechnics

Miss Potter is our English Teacher
Poetry's her forte
She has the knack of nouns
Her verbs leap from the page
Chased by crazy crackerjack adjectives
While adverbs burst brilliantly
Above their heads
In dazzling phrases
Like linguistic fireworks.
In Miss Potter's classes
We often have to wear
Sunglasses

When Miss Potter Asked Us to Write a Rap Poem

Yo,
Mr Fleming — did you admire
Those teachers who
Called you a liar?
Victorian teachers
Who hit you round the ear
Pushed you, pocked you
Taught you fear?
Made fun of your religion
Made fun of your nose
Made fun of your haircut
Made fun of your clothes
Detained you, caned you,
Hurt you, reviled you,
Taught you nothing about
Honesty, integrity
Taught you nothing but
What you *can't* do
Didn't even teach you
Anything half useful?
Yo, Mr Fleming
Did you think I too
Might one day
Be a teacher like you?
Carry a big stick
Always shout
Clever in a superficial
Artificial shallow mean

Official kind of way
Rap it out
Snap it out
You're gonna pay one day
Do you pray, Mr Fleming,
And were you ever young?
Were you born aged sixty
First step at sixty-one
Queued up at the window at sixty-two
To collect the living that
The world owed you
Is it true, Mr Fleming
That this is your creed?
I will *take* all that I need?
Aspire to dullness
And conformity
If you want creativity
Don't look at me
I will teach the children in my care
That life is a pain
That you have to bear
If I see a spark
Shining in their eyes
I will cover it and smother it
Until it dies
Sarcasm's my style and negativity
Wrapped in layers
Of narrow-minded bigotry.
Mr Flem, Flem, Fleming,
The last thing I say
Teachers like you
Got to fade away
You ain't a teacher

You're a full-blown
Fool
And we don't want teachers
Like you in school

The New Boy

Kevin Smart
New to the school
Dreadlocks
Clothes cool
Hangs loose
Hip-hop power
Built like
A power station
Cooling tower
Kevin Smart
Averts his eyes
His life is full
Of pain and lies
Eyes so sad
Won't meet your gaze
Lost in some Jamaican haze.
Kevin Smart
Cannot succeed
Put the boy
In Special Needs
Smart by name
But, sad to say,
I think it's best
Keep out his way

Going Mobile

I have a new toy
It's a mobile phone
I call it Eric
I have programmed it to play
Layla when it rings.
Mum says it's for emergencies only
So I've rung
Tommy, Des, Billy, Diane, Darren, Ali, Paul, Dom, Andrew, Sally
To tell them

I've got a message for Jenny, too.
J N Y I ♥ U
But Im 2 SCRD 2 → IT
(:-O

Head Teacher's Wise Words

Our head teacher said
That dogs live short lives
Compared to humans
Because they move
From sleep to action
So quickly

I asked if that was also
True of cows
Because
It sounded
Like bullocks
To me

Alarums Stage Left

Why does the firebell ring?
When Jenny and I
Are halfway through
An experiment to determine
(if she fancies me, really,
deep down)
The coefficient of expansion
Of various metals that
(she has a lovely figure
all curves
and light-brown hair
so soft
I can hardly keep from
Running my hands through …)
Ringringringringringringringring
Ringringringringringringringring
Ringringringringringringringring
Mr Paine yells
K-E-E-P C-A-L-M !
It's probably just a practice.
Leave your coats and bags and …
(His voice is drowned
In the noisy tide of Special Needs
Sweeping past like excited elks
In the corridor)
I hope it's a real fire, I say to Jenny.
Of course you don't, she retorts.
People would get hurt.
Smoke. Suffocation …
We join the flood of students

And I lose her in the jostle
And noisy chatter
We go Down the Up stairs
(Which in these circumstances
We're allowed to do)
But then I remember Tommy.
Where is he?
He'd never manage the crowd
With his leg in plaster.
And what if it's not a practice?
What if it's real?
I wait at the bottom of the stairs
Until the crowds have gone
And suddenly all is eerily deserted
And is it my imagination
Or can I smell smoke?
No sign of Tommy.
I rush up the stairs
Along the corridor.
I'm sure I can smell smoke.
And into the classroom.
Empty – just a slew of bags
And coats.
No Tommy!
I rush back down the stairs
And out on to the playground.
My class see me and they all cheer.
Mrs Taggart tut tuts.
And there's Tommy, grinning.

I went back for you, I yell,
In case it was a real fire.
I thought you'd need help!
It's okay, he said.
We went down the other stairs.
Jenny lent me
A hand

5: LOVE'S LABOURS

Jenny Let's Do It

Let's do it
Let's do it
Let's do it
Let's do it
Let's do it
Let's do it
Let's do it
Let's do it
Let's do it
Let's do it
Let's do it
Let's do it
Did you want to ask me something, Danny?
Er, yes, would you like
A lemonade?

Amplifier

Oh, amplifier
I love to stroke
Your silky-matt-black vinyl skin
To lightly turn your
Ergonomically shaped knobs
How I love your tiny red light
And almost inaudible hum
I thrill to the hollow click
As I plug in my guitar
Your voice, still soft, a little raspy
The big throaty scream
Of pleasurable pressure
As I hit the first chord

Fire Sign

(A song for Jenny — written on my new guitar.
I discovered that her birthday is in April and she's an Aries.
The song is based on A minor! Slow and moody.)

♫

I see your face in a ruby
Shining with a fire so bright
In your eyes are the burning stars
Lighting up the night

♫

And your lips are the deepest red
And your soul is the hottest hot
You've got love — it's a hundred per cent
I have to come back for another shot

♫

(Chorus)
You're a fire sign, baby.
Oh yes
A fire sign.
And you're gonna be
Mine.

♫

Your love is like a volcano
Smouldering hot and deep
You are the Phoenix in the flames
Rising through my sleep.

♫

Think you know all there is to know
Then she takes you by surprise
When she's gone you're walking in hell
When she's there you're in paradise

Repeat Chorus

Girl Talk

(Poem unfortunately found by Jenny
in my notebook and read by all her friends)
Girl talk
All about shopping
Hair
Eyeliner
Who's dating Namalee
What did Alyx say to Lee
Girl Talk
Make up
Shopping
Hair
Eyeliner
Who fancies Kerrie
What did Martin say to Emily
Girl talk
Make up
Shopping
Hair
Eyeliner
Boring as watching
A brick on a chair
Hair
Eyeliner
Chit chat
Soap dish
I sometimes wish
I was somewhere
Else

Boy Talk

(Written in my notebook
by Jenny Keane)
Boy talk
All about football
Who scored the goal
Cars
And bugger all
(Excuse my French)

I could say more
But please don't tempt me
It's basically
Their brains are empty!

The Detention Room

There are four thousand, one hundred
And ninety-four wall tiles
In the Detention Room

♫

There are twenty tables
Arranged in four rows of five
Facing the whiteboard
Facing north
Each table has a chipped surface
And several hard lumps of dried gum stuck
To its underside
In the Detention Room

♫

The door is in the east wall
Through the west windows
The sun sets over green fields
In the Detention Room

♫

Behind the teacher's desk
Is the whiteboard
By a trick of the light
Mr Fleming's shadow
Resembles a vulture
With a hatchet
In the Detention Room

♫

There is always screwed-up paper
Spent ink cartridges, crumpled cans
Crisp packets gathered in the back corners
Cobwebs
As though the cleaners
Are told never to clean
The Detention Room

♫

Ghosts of beaten boys
And abused girls hang becalmed
You can hear their desperate whisperings
Please, please
Release us from the Detention Room

♫

Thieves have lost their hands here
Drug pushers their noses
Rapists their balls
Murderers their brains
In the Detention Room

♫

Media studies filmed —
Marketing studies sold the concept —
Statisticians proved
That crime in schools doesn't pay
And that the Detention Room
Is no deterrent —
And the government crossed their ballot papers —
All here in the Detention Room

♫

Under cover of darkness
You can buy cigarettes here
You can buy drugs here
You can buy a gun here
For this is the Detention Room

For bringing Eric, my mobile phone, to school
Leaving it turned on
And playing *Layla* in Home Economics
I must spend the next forty minutes
Here in the Detention Room

6: CHRISTMAS CRACKER

Poem to Jenny (1)

I sit by the window
As the sky grows dark
Watching the road
From your house to the park

As you walk past the window
You see me and grin
I glance up – our eyes meet –
I wave – Come on in!

I open the front door
My face has gone red
I bring us two drinks
(There is much left unsaid)

There's a film at the Showcase
We both want to see
I suggest that we go there
You quickly agree

I sit by the window
The street lights come on
If you *had* passed – I wonder
What would I have done?

Poem to Jenny (2)

Jenny
Jenny
Jenny
Jenny
Jenny
Jenny
Jenny
Jenny
Jenny
Jenny
Jenny
Jenny
You don't seem
To notice me.

Poem to Jenny (3)

I'm very keen
On Jenny Keane

Video Nasty

I rented a disturbing video
And so the next day
I rented a turbing one
To cancel it out

Shelf Life

When my shelf collapsed
Under the weight of
All my poetry books
I repaired it as best I could
But it was
A shadow of its former shelf

Christmas in the Dark

Dad managed to put up
The Christmas decorations
Without mishap
But whilst hanging
The Christmas tree lights
Fused them
And all the lights
In the house

♫

Dad shouts at Mum
And says things I can't repeat
After a while
My eyes become accustomed
To the darkness
And then a flame bursts
Like a Bruce Willis explosion
And a candle lights up
Mum's all-suffering face
Like an old Italian painting
By Michelangelo
(Dad can be heard
banging about in the cellar,
still muttering unfortunate words)
There's a knock on the door
It's Mr Singh
From opposite.
All the lights in the street
Have gone out, he says.
Is your dad there?

Er, he's in the cellar,
Trying to mend a fuse.
No point, says Mr S.
It's the whole road.
(Oh no, I think,
Dad's fused the lights
In the whole road.)
Mr Singh leaves and Dad appears,
Still muttering
And clutching his arm
Where he banged into
The defunct fridge-freezer
In the dark
The phone rings.
I answer it.
It's Gran,
From the other side of town!
We're having a power cut, she says.
Who is it? asks Dad.
Gran!
What's she want?
Just to know if we're okay, I lie.
And then I wonder if the power cut
Has spread across the whole country
Or maybe the whole world
I go to the window
And gaze up at the sky
It's blank
No stars
Dad's done it now, I think

♫

And then at last

The lights blink back on
I notice that the sky is simply overcast
Mum is blowing out the candles
Dad is standing by the Christmas tree,
Deep in thought
Right, he says,
Let's have another go!

Her Royal Majesty

(written after watching the Queen's broadcast whilst eating Christmas dinner.)

♫

Queen,
Have you ever been
Down a mine?
And if you did
Was the coalface polished
To a right royal shine?

♫

Queen have you ever
Picked a bean?

♫

Have you ever been
On a bus?
Do you know what it's really like
To be one of us?

♫

Queen
Can you really, ever, truly know what I mean?

♫

(Princess Anne,
by the way,
I know you do what you can
For charity.
You're okay)

The Very Worst News

With a hint of nausea
As if I've been riding stormy seas
But haven't been anywhere near a boat
With slight indigestion
Thinking of the turkey carcass
That peers from the fridge
To gloat
Feeling chilly
Staring at the slate-grey sky
That refuses to snow
Or be at all seasonal
But only leaks tears
Feeling dizzy
And wishing
That while my parents were out
Visiting Auntie Jean I hadn't had
A few beers
I hear the bad news
Bad News
Like a seaside hotel with no sea views
Bad News
Like a crossword with no clues
Bad News
Pants too loose and too tight shoes
Bad News
When you never win and always lose
Really –
B-a-d N-e-w-s

Tommy rang to say
He'd had everything he wanted for Christmas
And what was that? I asked cheerily,
Not anticipating the kick in the shins
The sledgehammer blow to the head
The punch in the solar plexus
The meteorite about to obliterate the Earth
He said,
For Christmas I had
Jenny

7: THE YOUTH FACTORY CAN NEVER BE THE SAME AGAIN

The Playground

I am standing in the busy playground
But it feels like I'm alone
The sunlight is a rape-seed yellow
And the sky is an ice-field blue
Crisp leaves of dull brown and aching ochre
Rustle like a thousand paper flags
A white seagull and a black starling
Weave slo-mo circles, to and fro
A distant aeroplane departs
Glints like a star, waving farewell
The lemmings kick balls pointlessly,
Chasing shadows through the chill air
And low in the sky
Last night's heartless moon still hangs,
Pale now, and tired,
Gazing silently down
Upon my despair

Why?

Why is Kentucky Bluegrass green?
Why isn't Star Trek real?
Why does the Tower of Pisa lean?
Why can't I say how I feel?
Why are some films so bad you could weep?
And some films so good you don't want them to end?
And Jenny ...
Why didn't you accept my invitation?
The invitation I never found the courage to send?

Friends

Okay, Tommy,
Let's be friends again
It wasn't your fault
That Jenny made a play
For your dubious charms
And skill on the ball
I won't hold it against you
You got promoted
To the Premiership
I got demoted to Division Two
That's all

In Some Other Universe

In some other universe
A Danny Chaucer
Comes first
In the cross-country event
But I must admit
That in this universe
The Danny Chaucer
Thinks cross-country is
Shine shine
Sun sun shine
You ain't been shining
For a long long time

Cathy's Café

The bikers sprawl around
Slurping cappuccino
Listening to hard rock
That the jukebox plays
Eating eggs and bacon
In the stale haze of tobacco
Burnt grease and damp leather
At Cathy's Café

Me and Tommy shelter here
Because it's very close to
The cross-country route
Around which, on this day,
Our classmates are running
In this foul and freezing weather

(But we're all mates together
in Cathy's Café)

I Got The Blues So Bad

(My best song lyrics so far, I feel.)

♫

I got the blues so bad
I wanna crawl away and die
I got the blues so bad
I wanna crawl away and die
Feel like puking
Wanna crawl away and die

♫

I got the blues so bad
Gonna put my head down the toilet pan
I got the blues so bad
Gonna put my head down the toilet pan
Feel so bad
I ain't ever gonna feel good again

In The Wars

Tommy's been away
From school
Had to stay at home
To nurse his wounds
That's what the doctor said
Went to see Chelsea
Playing Liverpool away
Got in a fight
On the train coming home
He'd said, Better dead
Than red
Not the cleverest thing to say.

Struck by the Strangeness of Her Name

I was staring at a patch of wall
Half thinking about Forest
Half watching my breath spiral
Into the frosty air
And half thinking about
This afternoon's maths test
When I became aware
Of the girl standing beside me
I didn't recognise her —
In the year below me
I later discovered.
She said hello
And started chatting
I was struck by her beauty
Pale golden hair and skin
Winter-sun-bleached,
And by the strangeness of her name
Anastasia Aguilera
You play guitar, she said, smiling
(an interesting, cool and sexy
kind of smile)
I do
(I'd played in Lower School assembly once.
That must be how she knew)
I play bass.
My heart beat double time. *You do?*
I wonder if, she asked,
(Her eyes the palest blue)
If I could play with you?

8: IT'S ONLY ROCK 'N' ROLL BUT I'M RATHER FOND OF IT

Forming a Band

I said to Tommy Lock
I'm thinking of forming a band
Whaddya think?
Punk? He enquired
Boogie-woogie, Hip-hop?
70s influenced? Retro rock?
Acid-soul-house-jazz or pop?
Ambient-pyscho-techno-thrash?
Heavy metal? Hard core? Slash?
60s, flower-power, disco, soul?
I shrugged, *You know. Just rock 'n' roll.*

Wanted to Rock

The ad on the Music Department
Notice board read –
WANTED
Drummer and Keyboard player
For Exciting New Band
Influences Oasis
Travis
Blur
Deep Purple
And Led Zeppelin
(although Anastasia –
Anna for short –
thought that the inclusion
of the last two was rather sad
and wasn't sure if anyone
would have heard of them)
(Tho' Mr "Mickey" Most, Head of Music, had)

The Line-Up

Danny Chaucer
Lead guitar
Superstar

♫

Anastasia Aguilera
Bass
Ace

♫

Simon Scroggie
Drums
(Known as Scroggs)

♫

Morgan Pieniazczak
Keyboards
(The artiste formerly known as
Puny Moony)
(The artiste henceforth to be known as
Morgan the Organ)

Sticks and Stones
(and Other Possible Band Names)

The Well
Broken Elastica
Gulp
Old Leather
The Chemical Toilets
Trellis
Thin Girl Phat
The Plaster Casts
(suggested by Tommy)
Move Over Brahms
Smoke On The Water
(Suggested by Mickey Most)
Stairway to Shepherd's Bush
Some Might Say
That an Oasis title would be good
So that was settled –
Cast No Shadow

First Rehearsal

The first rehearsal
Took place in the music studio
Under the watchful eye of Mickey Most
Scroggs kept good time
On the school kit
And Morgan the Organ
Could play a bit
But then we hit a snag
There was one thing
Who was going to sing?
Morgan had a go
But sounded like somebody
Strangling a seal
(And anyway
Too nerdy for a front man)
Scroggs said
No way!
That wasn't in the deal
Well, I can't sing
Which left Anastasia
Who reluctantly agreed
To try
She sang
That old Oasis track
Don't Look Back In Anger
And – my oh my
She sang
Like an angel,
A voice drifting in the cosmos,
Ethereal, formless,

Shiver-down-the-spine

This band, said Scroggs,
is going to be
as big as West Coast Bound!
And who are they?
We all cried
Well, Scroggs replied,
They made 37 in the charts
In 1992 and had
A brilliant drum sound

Without Your Love

(The band are considering learning this. I haven't told them that it's about Anastasia. Haven't told Anastasia, either.)

♫

Without your love
I become so ordinary
Living in the commonplace
Living a common life

♫

But with your love
I become stronger than a speeding train
I can leap the universe
Not get wet in the rain

♫

Guess I'm a lucky man
Found what I was looking for
I found the key to the highway
I found the key to unlock your door

♫

Without your love
Without your love
I am nothing
Without your love
Without your love
I am a nobody
Just another face in the crowd

♫

For you are the woman of my dreams
We found each other in the storm
We rode the skyways
Now we're together in every new dawn

Latest Score

Tommy and Jenny
Are inseparable these days
And insufferable
How's your score, he asks
What?
Out of ten! He laughs
You know, three for a kiss,
Five up top ...
Oh, I don't know, I say
He winks
Eight! he says, expecting some response.
I nod, as if to say, so what, me too
He adds, *and a half!*

First Gig, New Love

Met her at the
Lower School Easter disco
On the penultimate day of term
Charlotte

♫

(Oh, oh, oh, Anastasia,
So sorry, you can't have me)
(Not that Anna knows I fancy her
We keep it strictly rock 'n' roll)

♫

Cast No Shadow were playing their first gig
Girls were screaming (honestly!)
Boys were transfixed by Anastasia's voice
And stage presence –
White tee shirt, tight white jeans
Slim body, white arms and face
Hair the palest spun gold
So vulnerable

♫

Some Year Eleven lads,
Des, Nez and Lee, who,
Strictly speaking,
Shouldn't have been there
Jeered, and laughed at Morgan,
But were hustled away
By Mickey Most and his (Year Twelve) posse
But I was hardly aware

Of anything, only the chords
Cutting air, my guitar riffs, the thrill
Of being there,
When ...

♫

Charlotte stood at the front
Small and slight
Black top, black skirt,
Black boots
Short black hair
Silver nose stud
Earrings (a selection)
Not my type but
Something about her

♫

She hung around while we packed away
She agreed to meet me on Saturday
Outside the ABC
I walked her to the bus stop
Kissed her in the shadows
Held her warm body close
Breathed her perfume
As my hands explored the warmth
Over her top,
No bra, my heart went
Boom, boom, boom!

She smiled
Kissed me lightly and was gone
I watched the bus
Swallowed by the night
What a first gig!
A-L-L R-I-G-H-T

A Close Call

In a quiet corner of the school field
Where the old boiler house
Meets the iron-spiked fence
And slugs and snails
Romp amongst the rotting leaves
Des, Nez and Lee
Gathered round a thin, bespectacled youth
And as I approached, I heard them say,
Think you can play?
He fancies himself
Puny Moony
Wimp – wants his mummy
Four eyes
Lard on a string
I knew I'd have to intervene
But was at a loss
What to do
If I wasn't careful
We'd both
End up with a kicking.
Except by chance, or fate
A third player in this drama was at hand
As the mighty shadow fell upon them
They looked up
Hello, Kevin, said Des
We were saying, said Nez
What a brilliant band that was
Last night, said Lee,
But with difficulty
As Kevin Smart

Was holding Lee by his lapels,
Suspending him mid-air,
As though he weighed no more
Than a box of staples
Treat Morgan with respect, okay?
They all nodded
TREAT MORGAN WITH RESPECT, OKAY?
They nodded even more
And swiftly walked away
And thus it was that Morgan lived to tell the tale
I was spared a difficult choice
(stand by my friend
or walk away alive)
A gang of Year Eleven bullies
Were quietly
Dissuaded from
An Act of Violence
And
Kevin Smart
Became the roadie for the band

9: CLOSE ENCOUNTERS

The Mystery of the Universe

That, I said,
Is the constellation of Orion
And that is his belt
Of silver and gold
Gazing at the galaxy
You feel so insignificant
The distances so vast
The stars so old

I pulled her close
Enjoying her frailty
Her warmth
She said
Can we go in now?
It's bleedin' cold

Charlotte's Sofa

The things Charlotte told me
I could hardly believe
A life of impossibilities
Sitting on her threadbare sofa
A couple of Woolworth's prints on the wall
TV blaring next door
Kids fighting upstairs

Her mum was friendly
Made us a cup of sweet tea
Left as alone
To talk
And explore one another's bodies
But Charlotte was not with me
Well, her body was, of course,
But not her mind
Her mind was somewhere else

We walked to the bus stop
Kissed goodbye
I sat on the bus
Half watching the dark shapes of factories
And shabby shops drift by
Half satisfied
Half wanting very much
To cry
I don't know why

Our Father
(for Charlotte)

Dear God,
If you exist
Tell Dad
Not to get too pissed

His skin is cratered
Nose is red
Please tuck him safely
Up in bed

Not roll home drunk
At half-past one
To take his anger
Out on Mum

By day our father
Is a gentle bloke
Dear God,
Is this some kind of joke?

Desolation Row

She lives
On the edge
Of the wasteland
In the shadow
Of broken-down dreams
The factories that once
Made life seem secure
Are coming apart
At the seams

She walks
Every day
To the bus stop
Boards the two twenty-two
In the rain
Says goodbye for the day
To the urban decay
But tonight
She will be
Back again

Graffiti

I am a modern artist
Picasso born again
My brush is a can of paint
My canvas is a train
I am written about in art books
I have found my claim to fame
A piece of art consisting
Solely of my name

The Old Science Block

The old science block is deserted
A few broken desks thick with dust
Bell jars covered in cobwebs
Bunsen burners covered in rust

♫

The wind blows through a hole in the window
Dried leaves weave a dance on the floor
Outside two voices are whispering
A key turns in the lock in the door

♫

Two figures appear in the doorway
And slowly walk into the gloom
Says the first, *It was fate, don't you reckon,
Finding the key to this room?*

♫

They go through to the old science storeroom
Shelves, once full of treasures, now sag
Under the weight of old memories
And a box with a sleeping bag

♫

Warning – Do not touch this equipment
The bag's laid out under the sign
Are you sure that it's safe? asks Jenny.
Says Tommy, *It will be fine*

♫

The old science block is deserted
A few broken desks thick with dust
Bell jars covered in cobwebs
Bunsen burners covered in rust

Rhythmic Breakdown

I sent my love a letter
I sent the letter **Y**
She sent me back a letter
And this was her witty reply
I'm sorry but I no longer
Wish to go out with you

We Split Up Due to Musical Differences

She said
She'd rather be squashedtoapapthanlistento
Pulp
(gulp!)

♫

She said
She'd rather be droppedfromaplaneintherainintheForest-
ofDeanthanlistento
Ocean Colour
Scene

♫

She said
She'd rather blowherownheadoffwithacannonfromtwo-
pacesthanlistento

♫

I said
Goodbye

After the Party

Our relationship was clearly over
Nevertheless
I waited with her at the bus stop
But there was nothing left to say

pom di do

(whistle)

di dum
di dah

(sigh)

tum ti tay

10: SWEET SOUL MUSIC

Canteen Encounter

Across a crowded dining hall
I glimpse Anna
In a golden spotlight
Moving in slow motion
Ballerina-like
Between the tables
Despite the distance and the hubbub
She seems to sense
My presence
And glances up quickly
Catching my eye
I look away at my tray
And then say
To the dinner lady,
A *cheeseburger, chips and peas*
Please

Light Haiku

I saw a black sky
Above the alien earth
And I was alone

You entered my life
The universe erupted
A billion stars

Indeed I Do

(Written for Anna to sing. But no tune yet.)
I need you
Like a flower needs the rain
Indeed I do
Without you I'd go insane
I need you
Indeed I do

♫

I need you
To hold me tight
Indeed I do
In the morning, in the night
I need you
Indeed I do

♫

Needing you so bad
Needing you so bad
When I'm with you
I have the best time
That a girl ever had
Indeed I do

♫

I need you
Like a ship needs the sea
Indeed I do
Say you'll sail home to me
I need you
Indeed I do

When the Words Meet the Melody

After school
The music block is deserted
(a rare occurrence)
as Anna and I prepare
to run through
a couple of new songs
Look, I say,
And bring out my folder
Of lyrics
Her slender fingers
Turn the pages
Her face concentrates
For some reason
I feel nervous
I'm sweating
She takes *Indeed I Do*
And places it on the piano
I didn't know you could play, I say
She plays a chord progression
That I've never heard
She sings
Her voice makes me shiver
The voice of a lost soul
All the beauty of the world
Rolled into a single sound
Transforming my boring
Mundane lyrics
Ordinary words
To extraordinary emotions
The song ends

What do you think? she asks
I've had that melody for a while
I can't think of words that
Adequately describe how I feel
So I say — *Great! Brilliant!*
Mickey Most appears
Nice tune, he comments. *What band did that?*
<u>We</u> wrote it, I say proudly
He glances at the clock.
Right. Sorry, I'm going to have to
Turf you two out
I've got to lock up early tonight

Heatwave

It's so hot, said Anna,
That the lampposts are melting
And the pavements
Are turning to treacle
It's so hot, I said,
That they're airlifting an iceberg
From Iceland
To drop into the school pool
It's so hot, said Morgan,
That cars are spontaneously
Bursting into flame
Well, said Scroggs,
I'm thinking of trying
Some heavier drumsticks

Beneath the Spreading Chestnut Tree

Anna and I
Sit in cool black shadow
Beneath a spreading chestnut tree
In the corner
Of the school field
Hiding from the sticky
Lunchtime heat
And talking, as always,
About *Cast No Shadow*
It will soon be
The school
End of term gig
And a local agent
Who can get the band work
Will be coming
Anna's mum
Has access to a van
And so the plan
For world and
Chart domination
Is coming together

♫

Anna lies back
On the soft grass
Shielding her eyes from the sun
She tells me
That her dad left home
When she was three

Maybe she remembers him
Maybe she only remembers
A photograph
Almost without thinking
I do the very thing
I've dreamed of doing
For so long
But have never
Plucked up courage to do
On impulse, I bend forward
And kiss her lips
For a delicious moment
She responds –
Then gently moves her head away
And smiles
You're very sweet, she tells me,
But let's not spoil a good thing
Let's just stay
Good friends –
And the world's
Most successful songwriting
Partnership ever
I nod, and do my best
To smile
Of course, I say,
Just good friends

Don't Touch Blues

(A twelve bar in the key of E. Not really a song for the band.)

♪

You can look
But don't touch
You can look
But don't touch
You can look
But you better not touch
You can look
But don't touch
You can look
But don't touch
You. can look
But you better not touch
You can look
But don't touch
You can look
But don't touch
Anna, baby,
I need you so much

11: FADE AFTER LAST CHORUS

The Agent and the End of Term Gig

What a gig!
The best we'd ever played
Sensational!
The crowd went wild.
Anna was a rock icon!
Her voice raised the dead
The audience started to weep,
Lashing themselves into a frenzy
With crazy string
The drums were a herd
Of wildebeest
Charging down a ravine
My guitar licks would have caused Clapton
To lay down his axe and take up sewing
Morgan's organ soared into the ionosphere
And the sound was astounding
Thanks to Kevin Smart
Who it transpires *is* special
At twiddling the knobs
In short
Each song was a masterpiece.
And the agent
Who was coming to see us,
Bringing us gigs
Across the width
And breadth of the land
Didn't turn up

♫

Said Anna to me,

Oh well,
C'est la vie
Said Morgan
Oh dear
C'est la guerre
With Anna
I had to agree
With Morgan
I had to concur

End of School

As the school streams out of the school gates
For the last time this term
I wait
For Anna
There is a flash of light
And she appears
I thought we might get together
In the holidays, I say
She sighs, smiles, shakes her head,
Sorry, I'd love to – but not possible
A cloud blots out the sun
I thought we could write some new songs
She shrugs. *No, I'm sorry. I can't*
The sky is grey now, and it's growing darker
I thought we'd rehearse, I say
Well, the band can, but I won't be there
A few spots of rain fall
And somebody cheers
You're not leaving the band are you? I ask
Beginning to panic
She laughs. *Of course not!*
Just going away for the summer
She holds my hand
There's an enormous clap of thunder
That shakes the ground
Don't be silly. The band
Is going to be the biggest in the land
Remember?
Mum says she'll sort us out some gigs
It'll be great

Don't worry
Just keep the others up to scratch
And I'll see you in September
She kisses me lightly
There is a crack of lightning
And she is gone

I stand in the cool rain
Thinking about *Cast No Shadow*
For the first time I'm
Looking forward to next term
My thoughts are interrupted
By the braying laughter of a fire engine
And the wounded cry of an ambulance
Scroggs appears, out of breath
The old science block
Has been hit by lightning,
He gasps
The roof fell in
And Tommy was inside

A Long Time
(Song for Anna)

It's gonna be a long time
Waiting for you
To come back to me
It's gonna be a long time
And I
Can only count the days

♫

Counting the days
Watching the sun
Circling the sky
Counting the ways
That I
Love you

♫

It's gonna be a long time
Waiting for you to do
What you have to do
It's gonna be a long time
'Til we
Are together again

♫

Together again
In the sun or the rain
And I
Can love you
Once again

It's gonna be a long time
'Til I
Can love you again.

News From the Hospital

Well, Tommy, I said
At his hospital bed
Perusing his bruises and cuts
A narrow escape
Let me peel you a grape
And open that bag of nuts

♫

Says Tommy to me,
It's not easy
To tell you what I have to say
It's all about me and Jenny
We heard she was pregnant today

Unicorn

I climb from my dream and walk in silence
From the streets of my childhood
To the field beneath the stars
Where I softly say the magic word
That calls the unicorn

I jump on to his broad white back
I feel his muscles rippling
And the thunder of his hooves on the grass
As dark blue shadows rush beneath us

We rise towards the burning stars
I feel the cool moonshine on my cheek
And the world seems so small beneath me
I could reach down and pick it up

We have left my past behind
And I know with certainty
That my universe is forever changed
And in the brightest star I see a baby's face

When I wake in the morning
I gaze up at the brand new sky
Thinking of Tommy and Jenny
And I see the passing of the unicorn
As vapour trails across the heavens

Long Haul Flight

A glint of silver
Like a star
Lost in a vast expanse of blue
A soft rumble
And a trace of vapour trail
Anastasia in the window seat
Peers down
Finally spotting the Youth Factory,
Tiny and insignificant
She smiles to herself and,
Even though nobody below
Can see her,
She waves and blows me a kiss
Au revoir, Danny, she whispers
Or at least
I imagine that's how it goes